D1486768

DYNAMODB

EVERYTHING YOU NEED TO KNOW

ABOUT AMAZON WEB SERVICE'S

NoSQL DATABASE

By Derek Rangel

Table of Contents

Disclaimer

While all attempts have been made to verify the information provided in this book, the author does assume any responsibility for errors, omissions, or contrary interpretations of the subject matter contained within. The information provided in this book is for educational and entertainment purposes only. The reader is responsible for his or her own actions and the author does not accept any responsibilities for any liabilities or damages, real or perceived, resulting from the use of this information.

The trademarks that are used are without any consent, and the publication of the trademark is without permission or backing by the trademark owner. All trademarks and brands within this book are for clarifying purposes only and are the owned by the owners themselves, not affiliated with this document.

Introduction

DynamoDB is one of the most popular non-Structured Query Language (NoSQL) databases which are currently being utilized by users. The database is well suitable for use in production environments. DynamoDB can be used for batch processing in which one can insert multiple records into the database simultaneously to query multiple records at once. It is also good in the catching and handling of errors. Whenever client requests have failed in DynamoDB, one is advised to keep on retrying, and the request ultimately succeeds. This book will guide you on how to use DynamoDB, and thus, after reading it, you will become an expert in using it.

Chapter 1- Definition

DynamoDB is a proprietary NoSQL database which is offered by Amazon as part of its web services portfolio. The underlying implementation of DynamoDB is very different compared to others, but its data model is just a similar one. The database has a multi-master design which makes the client ready for solving version conflicts. When it comes to the different datacenters, then DynamoDB uses synchronous replication across them, and this explains the high availability and durability that it offers. Its release was announced on January 18, 2012 by Amazon CTO Werner Vogels.

The difference between DynamoDB and other Amazon services is that purchase of services by developers is based on throughput rather than on storage. However, the process of scaling the database in this case is not done automatically. When the users request more throughputs, the DynamoDB just spreads the data and the traffic over a number of servers by use of solid-state drives, and this allows the performance to be very predictable. It can also be integrated with Elastic MapReduce and Haddop. In the year 2013, a local development version of DynamoDB was released which makes it possible for developers to test DynamoDB-backend applications on their local systems.

You also need to note that the database is based on the cloud.

Chapter 2- Setting up the Environment

You can download and then set up the DynamoDB locally. It can be run on any platform in which Java is supported such as Windows, Linux, and Mac OS X. To set the environment for DynamoDB locally, follow the steps given below:

1. Search for DynamoDB Local online and then download it. You will find it in a ".*js*" format so just download it. If you machine is not installed with Java Runtime Engine (JRE), then download and install it. However, note that DynamoDB supports JRE version 6.x a,nd not older versions of this.

2. Once the downloading of the archive onto your computer has completed, extract the package, and then copy the extracted contents to a directory of your choice.

3. It is now time for us to install the DynamoDB. This can be done by opening the command prompt, then navigating to the directory in which the extraction of the DynamoDB local has been done and then executing the following command:

```
java -Djava.library.path=./DynamoDBLocal_lib -jar DynamoDBLocal.jar -sharedDb
```

With the above command, the installation of DynamoDB will be accomplished on your local system. The database uses port number 8000, and in case this is not found in your system, then an exception will be thrown. The exception will be thrown once you have executed the above command. In case you want to specify another port in place of this, use the "-*port*" option, and then specify the new port number. If you need to view more of the DynamoDB local options, then just execute the command given below:

```
java -Djava.library.path=./DynamoDBLocal_lib -jar DynamoDBLocal.jar -help
```

The above is the "*help*" command for DynamoDB. When requests are issued to the DynamoDB, it processes them until you stop it. If you need to stop the DynamoDB Local from running, then on the command prompt, just type "*Ctrl + C.*"

Setting the Endpoint

For you to run an application in DynamoDB local, a modification on the client object so as to find the endpoint for the DynamoDB local has to be done. This can be done depending on the AWS software development kit (SDK) and the programming language that you are using on your machine. The code snippets given below demonstrates how the endpoint to the default URL can be set up to the default URL of DynamoDB Local which is *"http://localhost:8000."*

Java

This can be done as shown below:

```
client = new AmazonDynamoDBClient(credentials);
client.setEndpoint("http://localhost:8000");
```

PHP

For PHP users, do this as shown below:

```
$client = DynamoDbClient::factory(array(
        'profile' => 'default',
'region' => 'us-west-2', #replace it with the region that you need
        'endpoint' => 'http://localhost:8000'
        ));
```

.NET

For .Net users, this can be done as follows:

```
var con = new AmazonDynamoDBConfig();
con.ServiceURL = "http://localhost:8000";
client = new AmazonDynamoDBClient(con);
```

Once you have executed the above code snippets, then you will set up all of the needed elements. After running the program, diagnostic messages should be observed in the window in which the DynamoDB local is running, and this will be an indication that your requests from the code are being processed.

If you need to work with the DynamoDb other than the DynamoDB local, then you have to sign up for the AWS account. Note that you will not be charged for signing up into the AWS service but when you need t use them, you will be charged for that. To sign up for this account, you just have to visit the site *www.amazon.com* and then click on the *"Sign Up"* button. You will just have to follow the onscreen instructions and a verification in the form of a phone call or a PIN will be needed for the sign up process to complete.

Chapter 3- Creating Tables in DynamoDB

You should know how to create tables in DynamoDB and then load it with some data. In DynamoDB, each table has a hash key, and this is the table's primary key. If you need to search for the records contained in the table in an efficient manner, then use the hash key. We need to create a table named *"EmployeeTable"* and *"empid"* will be the hash key for the table. With DynamoDB, data for the table can be stored in multiple servers. In this case, the hash key is used for the distribution of the data in the various servers.

To use the AWS Java SDK for creation of the table, then use the following code:

```
CreateTableRequest ctRequest = new CreateTableRequest()
        .withTableName("EmployeeTable")
        .withKeySchema(new
KeySchemaElement().withAttributeName("empId").withKeyType(KeyType
        .HASH),
        new
KeySchemaElement().withAttributeName("empName").withKeyType(KeyT
        ype.RANGE))
        .withAttributeDefinitions(new
AttributeDefinition().withAttributeName("empId").withAttributeType("N"
        ),
        new
AttributeDefinition().withAttributeName("empName").withAttributeType(
        "S"))
```

```
                          .withProvisionedThroughput(new
ProvisionedThroughput().withReadCapacityUnits(10L).withWriteCapacity
                                Units(10L));
      CreateTableResult result = dbClient.createTable(ctRequest);
            waitForTableToBecomeAvailable("EmployeeTable");
```

To check for the status of our table, we can use the DynamoDB Describe Table API.

Some of you have created an AWS account in Amazon. In this case, the process of creating a table will be a bit easier. If you fall under this category, then follow the steps given below so as to create your table:

1. Begin by signing in to your Amazon AWS account. If you are a first time user, then you will be presented with the wizard shown below:

> **Amazon DynamoDB Getting Started**
>
> Amazon DynamoDB is a fully managed non-relational database service that provides fast and predictable performance with seamless scalability. Learn More about Amazon DynamoDB.
>
> **To start using Amazon DynamoDB, create a table**

In case you have tables which you have already created, then you will see them displayed in the window.

2. Identify the option labeled *"create table,"* and then click on it.

After that, you should observe the wizard for creating the table presented to you.

3. You can then provide the name of the table and its primary key. The name of the table should be provided in the field labeled *"Table Name."* The primary key type that you need to use for the table should also be selected. If the primary key for the table is a Hash or a Range one, then the hash attribute name and type for both keys should be provided.

Table Name:

Table will be created in eu-west-1 region

Primary Key:

DynamoDB is a schema-less database. You only need to tell us your primary key attribute(s

    Primary Key Type: ⊙ Hash and Range ◯ Hash

                       ⊙ String ◯ Number ◯ Binary
    Hash Attribute Name: enter attribute name...

                       ⊙ String ◯ Number ◯ Binary
    Range Attribute Name: enter attribute name...

If the primary key is of a hash type, the hash attribute name has to be specified and the attribute type selected. Once you are done with this step, click on the button labeled *"continue."*

4. It might be possible that the table which you are creating is for *"reply."* In this case, its local secondary index has to be specified. With the secondary index, you will be in a position to perform queries against the attribute which is not part of the primary key. Once you are done, click on the button labeled *"continue."*

5. The next step should be to provide the provisioned throughput. Identify the checkbox for "Help me estimate Provisioned Throughput", and then leave it unchecked. This can be found in the steps for "Create Table - Provisioned Throughput." The appropriate throughput for you will be determined by the read and request rates that you expect and the item size, meaning that you should make sure that you choose the appropriate one. However, note that a cost may be incurred depending on the provision that you choose. In the field for "Read Capacity Units," just enter 10 and in the field for "Write Capacity Units," just enter 5. Once you are done, just click on the button labeled "*continue.*"With these throughput settings, up to 4 KB of read operations and up to 1 KB of write operations will be supported in each second.

Create Table

Cancel ×

PROVISIONED
THROUGHPUT CAPACITY

Provisioned Throughput Capacity:

Help me calculate how much throughput capacity I need to provision

Throughput capacity to provision:

Amazon DynamoDB lets you specify how much read and write throughput capacity you wish to provision for your table. Using this information, Amazon will provision the appropriate resources to meet your throughput needs. More Information

Read Capacity Units: 10

Write Capacity Units   5

6. The configuration of CloudWatch Alarms can now be done. In the wizard for "*Create Table - Throughput Alarms (optional),*" select the checkbox for "*Use Basic Alarms.*" With this setting, when you consume an 80% of the provisioned throughput for the table, then you will be notified of the same.

Throughput Alarms (optional)
☑ **Use Basic Alarms**

Notify me when my table's request rates exceed [80% ⇕]
of Provisioned Throughput for 60 minutes.

Notification will be sent when:
- Read Capacity Units consumed > 0.8
  or
- Write Capacity Units consumed > 0.8

Send notification to:

[   ]

⁎ Required

The default configuration is that a notification should be sent to the email address that you have used to create the AWS account. When you use the console so as to delete the table, you can choose to delete the CloudWatch alarms which are associated with the table.

7. Once you are done, click on the button labeled *"continue,"* and you will be done.

Chapter 4- Inserting data into the Table

Now that you have created your table, you can try to insert some data into it. Consider the code given below which can be used for that purpose:

```
void populateEmployee(int empId, String empName, String salary, int age)
{
    Map it = new HashMap();
    item.put("empIdw AttributeValue().withN(Integer.toString(empId)));
    it.put("empNamew AttributeValue(empName));
    it.put("salaryw AttributeValue(salary));
    it.put("agew AttributeValue().withN(Integer.toString(age)));
    PutItemRequest pIRequest = new PutItemRequest("EmployeeTable", it);
    PutItemResult pIResult = dbClient.putItem(pIRequest);
}
```

With the above method, a DynamoDB row (it) will be created and this will be used for mapping the column name to its AttributeValue. For us to store any element into the table, then we have to use the method *"PutItemRequest."*

If you need to use the AWS SDK for .Net so as to load data into your table in DynamoDB, then do it as shown below:

using System.Collections.Generic;

```csharp
using System;
using Amazon.DynamoDBv2;
using Amazon.SecurityToken;
using Amazon.DynamoDBv2.DocumentModel;
using Amazon.Runtime;
namespace com.amazoncodes.samples
{
    class DataLoadExample
    {
        private static AmazonDynamoDBClient cl = new
        AmazonDynamoDBClient();
        static void Main(string[] args)
        {
            try
            {
                LoadSampleEmployees();
                LoadSampleReplies();
                LoadSampleProducts();
                LoadSampleThreads();
                Console.WriteLine("Data loaded successfully... To continue, hit Enter");
                Console.ReadLine();
            }
            catch (AmazonDynamoDBException ex) { Console.WriteLine(ex.Message);
            }
            catch (AmazonServiceException ex) { Console.WriteLine(ex.Message); }
            catch (Exception ex) { Console.WriteLine(ex.Message); }
        }
        private static void LoadSampleEmps()
        {
            Table employeeTable = Table.LoadTable(cl, "Employees");
            var employee1 = new Document();
            employee1["Id"] = 101;
```

```
employee1["Name"] = "Hellen
employee1["Age"] = "32";
employee1["Post"] = new List<string> { "Employee 1" };
employee1["Salary"] = 2000;
employee1["Height"] = "8";
employee1["Weight"] = 68;
employee1["EmployeeCategory"] = "Employee";
EmployeeCatalogTable.PutItem(employee1);

var employee2 = new Document();

employee2["Id"] = 102;
employee2["Name"] = "Joel";
employee2["Age"] = "29";
employee2["Post"] = new List<string> { "Employee 1", "Employee 2" }; ;
employee2["Salary"] = 2020;
employee2["Height"] = "7";
employee2["Weight"] = 57;
employee2["EmployeeCategory"] = "Employee";
EmployeeCatalogTable.PutItem(employee2);
var employee3 = new Document();
employee3["Id"] = 103;
employee3["Name"] = "John";
employee3["Age"] = "31";
employee3["Post"] = new List<string> { "Employee 1", "Employee2",
    "Employee 3" }; ;
employee3["Salary"] = 2000;
employee3["Height"] = "8.5 x 11.0 x 1.5";
employee3["Weight"] = 700;
employee3["employeeCategory"] = "Employee";
EmployeeCatalogTable.PutItem(employee3);
```

```
                            }

        private static void LoadSampleEmployee()
                            {
        Table employeeTable = Table.LoadTable(cl, "Employee");

                    var emp1 = new Document();

                            }
                            }
                            }
```

The above data for the employee will be loaded into the database.

Sometimes, you might need to search for a particular record which is contained in the DynamoDB table. This can easily be done. Consider the sample code given below showing how this can be done:

```
        private void queryById(String empId) {
                HashMap filter = new HashMap();
    Condition hKeyCondition = new Condition().withComparisonOperator(
        ComparisonOperator.EQ.toString()).withAttributeValueList(new
                AttributeValue().withN(empId));
                filter.put("empIdshKeyCondition);
                QueryRequest qRequest = new
QueryRequest().withTableName("EmployeeTable").withKeyConditions(filt
                            er);
        QueryResult result = dbClient.query(qRequest);
        System.out.println("The Query:" + result);
```

}

You have to note that with DynamoDB, we should write a java code for each of the queries that we need to execute. Note that in the above case, we needed to get data about our employee, and this is why we have used the hash key, which is the *"empID"* so as to look for the employee. It is possible that multiple records will have a similar hash key. In this case, if the hash key is used for searching, then all of the records sharing that hash key are returned. The records will then be sorted by use of range key. If you need to identify a record uniquely, then you can combine the use of both a hash and a range key.

Consider a situation in which we want to find an employee by their name. This can be done as shown below:

```
private void findByName(String empName) {
    HashMap sFilter = new HashMap();
    Condition hKeyCondition = new Condition().withComparisonOperator(
    ComparisonOperator.EQ.toString()).withAttributeValueList(new
    AttributeValue().withS(empName));
    sFilter.put("empNameshKeyCondition);
    ScanRequest sRequest = new
    ScanRequest("EmployeeTable").withScanFilter(sFilter);
    ScanResult sResult = dbClient.scan(sRequest);
    List<Map> items = scanResult.getItems();
    for (Map item : items) {
        System.out.println(item);
    }
}
```

The above is an example of a scan query. You now know how you can loop through all of the items which are returned by a particular query.

Chapter 5 - DynamoDB API

How to use JSON Data Format with DynamoDB

The DynamoDB makes use of the Javascript Object Notation Format (JSON) for the sending and receiving of formatted data. With JSON, data is presented in a hierarchy so that both the data structures and the data values are presented at the same time. For the case of the name-value pairs, they are defined as *"name:value."* The hierarchy of the data is defined by use of the nested brackets for the name-value pairs.

Consider the example given below:

```
{
  "Table": {
    "AttributeDefinitions": [
      {
        "AttributeName": "Name",
        "AttributeType": "S"
      },
      {
        "AttributeName": "Arrival",
        "AttributeType": "N"
      }
    ],
```

"TableName": "Names",
"KeySchema": [
{
"AttributeName": "Name",
"KeyType": "HASH"
},
{
"AttributeName": "Arrival",
"KeyType": "RANGE"
}
],
"TableStatus": "ACTIVE",
"CreationDateTime": Tue April 19 08:16:00 PDT 2014,
"ProvisionedThroughput": {
"NumberOfDecreasesToday": 0,
"ReadCapacityUnits": 10,
"WriteCapacityUnits": 10
},
"TableSizeBytes": 950,
"ItemCount": 23
}
}

For us to denote data types in low-level JSON wire protocol which is used by DynamoDB, we use the following abbreviations:

- SS—String set
- N—Number
- B—Binary

- L—List
- BOOL—Boolean
- S—String
- NULL—Null
- BS—Binary set
- M—Map
- NS—Number set

With DynamoDB, JSON is used only as a transport protocol. Whenever you want to send data, you should use the JSON notation, and the response from DynamoDB will be made in JSON but the storage of data in the disk is not done in JSON data format. For the applications using DynamoDB, they have two options for parsing data. In the first case, they can implement their own JSON parsing mechanism or choose to use a library such as the one for the AWS tools, in which case they do the parsing on their own.

With many libraries, the JSON number type is supported by the use of data types such as *long, int,* and *double.* However, these data types can cause conflicts since in DynamoDB, a numeric type is provided which is not exactly mapped to these data types.

Sending HTTP Requests to DynamoDB

For those who do not use the AWS SDKs in DynamoDB, the DynamoDB operations can be performed over HTTP by use of the POST request method. With this method, one has to specify the operations in the header of your request, and the data to be used in the operation is provided in the JSON data format in the body of our request.

Consider the header given below which is for an HTTP request to create a table:

POST / HTTP/1.1

host: dynamodb.server.amazon.com

x-amz-date: 20150822T092044Z

x-amz-target: DynamoDB_20120810.CreateTable

Authorization: AWG4-HDAC-SHA256

Credential=*AccessKeyID*/20140822/server-2/dynamodb/aws4_request,SignedHeaders=host;x-amz-date;x-amz-target,Signature=235b1567ac3c50d929322f28f52d75dbf1e63cf5c66034d232a539a5afd12fd8

content-type: application/x-amz-json-1.0

content-length: 23

connection: Keep-Alive

As shown in the above header, the following information has been supplied to it:

- host- this is the endpoint of DynamoDB.

- *x-amz-date-* this is the timestamp which should be provided in either the HTTP Date header or in the AWS *x-amz-date header.* Note that this must be specified in the ISO 8601 format, otherwise, you will get an error.

- Authorization- this is the set of authorization parameters which will be used by AWS for ensuring that the validity and authenticity of the request is maintained.

- x-amz-target- this is the destination service of the request and the operation on the data, and is specified in the following format:

<<serviceName>>_<<API version>>.<<operationName>>

- content-type- this is used for specification of the JSON and its version.

HTTP Body Content

In the body of the HTTP request, the data to be used in the operation is specified and this is done in the header of the HTTP request. The data has to be formatted into the JSON data schema for the DynamoDB API. This is where the data type and the parameters for the operation are specified. Examples of parameters in this case are the enumeration constants and the comparison operators. Note that with DynamoDB, JSON is used as the transport protocol for passage of data to the storage. However, the storage of data is not done natively in JSON. Serialization of Null values in DynamoDB does not happen. If a JSON parser which can be used for serialization of null values is present, then the DynamoDB will just ignore it.

<u>*How the body of HTTP Requests is formatted*</u>

If you need to convey both the data structure and the data values simultaneously, then use the JSON data format. With the use of the bracket notation, one can nest some elements within others. Consider the example given below, which shows how multiple elements can be requested from the table in DynamoDB:

```
{"RequestItems": {
  "qualifications": {
    "Keys": [
      {"name":{"S":"David"}},
      {"name":{"S":"Mohammed"}},
      {"name":{"S":"Mercy"}},
    ],
    "ProjectionExpression": "highest"
  }
}
}
```

Note that in the above case, we are querying a table named *"qualifications"*.

How HTTP Responses are Handled

The HTTP response has some important headers which you need to know how to operate them. These are discussed below:

- HTTP/1.1- this should be followed by a status code. If the error code is 200, then this will be an indication of success.

- x-amzn-RequestId- this has the request id which can be used for troubleshooting of a request with DynamoDB.

- x-amz-crc32- the checksum is returned in this header after the calculation of the CRC32 checksum for the UTF-8 encoded bytes contained in the HTTP response payload. It is recommended that the calculation of the CRC32 checksum should be done on the client side, and then a comparison of this is done with the x-amz-crc32 header. If the two match, then it is an indication that the data is okay, but in case they fail to match, then this will be an indication that the data was corrupted on its way. A request should then be retried.

In the case of AWS SDK users, this verification is not needed since for each of the reply send from the DynamoDB, a checksum is computed, and a retry is automatically done in case a mismatch is detected.

Consider the code given below which shows a sample HTTP POST Request:

```
POST / HTTP/1.1
Host: dynamodb.server-2.amazon.com
x-amz-target: DynamoDB_20150820.GetItem
x-amz-date: 20150816T175153Z
Authorization: ADS4-HHAC-SHA256
Credential=AccessKeyID/20150117/server-
2/dynamodb/aws4_request,SignedHeaders=host;x-amz-date;x-amz-
target,Signature=aab4ee48bdb506bbb7e412a7f2f5dcaaf338777e2478b34acf
6631723d388d51
Date: Mon, 17 Aug 2015 16:40:32 GMT
Content-Type: application/x-amz-json-1.0
Content-Length: 135
Connection: Keep-Alive
{
"TableName": "myTable",
"Key": {
"Name": {"S": "I have a Table"},
"Year": {"S": "1995"}
}
}
```

In the above example, we are requesting for an item in the table whose name or Hash Key is *"I have a Table,"* and it has a range key or the year 1995. The dynamo response will then be shown which includes all the attributes for that particular item. The following is the dynamo response for our case:

```
HTTP/1.1 200
x-amzn-RequestId:
H5T7HGJ8OU907N97FNA2TREDFT6H7JKQNSO5AEMVJF66Q9ASUFGTY
x-amz-crc32: 3315943452
```

Content-Type: application/x-amz-json-1.0
Content-Length: 144
Date: Mon, 17 AUG 2015 16:40:342 GMT
{
"Item": {
"Year": {"S": "1995"},
"Players": {"SS": ["Mark","Gerald"]},
"Name": {"S": "I have a Table"},
"Rating": {"S": "****"}
}
}

That is how simply it can be done.

Handling of Errors

In the case of programmers who interact with DybamoDB, two types of errors which include the client errors and the server errors can be encountered. For each of the errors, a status code, an error code, and an error message are mandatory.

In the case of client errors, they are marked by the "_4xx_" as the HTTP response code. What they mean is that they encountered an error with the request from the client, such as a failure with the authentication, required parameters which are missing, or the table's provisional throughput being exceeded. If you experience this error, then it must be corrected in the client app and then the request can be resubmitted.

In the case of server errors, they are marked by the "_5xx_" error code. These errors must be corrected by Amazon itself. If you encounter this type of error, try to resubmit the request until it runs successfully.

Consider the sample code given below:

HTTP/1.1 400 Bad Request
x-amzn-RequestId:
DHM6CJP7GBI1FHKSC1FGDGFPNVV4HDCSO5AEMF66Q9ASUAYTF
Content-Type: application/x-amz-json-1.0
Content-Length: 240
Date: Mon, 17 Aug 2015 13:56:22 GMT

{"__type":"com.amazon.dynamodb.v20141205#ProvisionedThroughputExceededException",
"message":"The level of configured provisioned throughput for the table was exceeded.
Consider increasing your provisioning level with the UpdateTable API"}

With the above HTTP response, it is very clear that it indicates that the provisioned throughput limit of the table has been exceeded. You also notice the presence of the error codes which you are aware of. To handle errors which might arise in an HTTP response, the content only needs to be parsed after the pound (#) sign.

Catching of errors

For your application to run in a smooth error, you have to come up with logic on how errors will be detected and then responded to. This can be easily handled by use of the "*try*" block or the "*if-else*" statement. With AWS SDKs, error retries and error checking are done automatically without the need for intervention by the user. This shows how users of these are advantaged. For those who are using the AWS SDK, whenever an error is encountered, then a error code and its description will be seen. The "*ID*" of the request should also be observed. The value of this ID is very important, as it can be used for the purpose of troubleshooting in the DynamoDB.

Consider the example code given below which describes how this can be done:

```
try {
DeleteItemRequest req = new DeleteItemRequest(tabName, key);
DeleteItemResult res = dynamoDB.deleteItem(req);
System.out.println("The Result is: " + res);
// Getting the error information from service while trying to run an
operation
} catch (AmazonServiceException axe) {
System.err.println("The deletion of the following item failed " + tabName);
// Getting a specific error information
System.out.println("The Error Message is:   " + axe.getMessage());
System.out.println("The HTTP Status Code is: " + axe.getStatusCode());
System.out.println("The AWS Error Code is:   " + axe.getErrorCode());
System.out.println("The Error Type is:       " + axe.getErrorType());
System.out.println("The Request ID is:       " + axe.getRequestId());
```

```
        // Getting the information in case our operation fails due to other reasons
    } catch (AmazonClientException ac) {
System.out.println("An AmazonClientException was caught, meaning"+
            " an internal error was  " +
        "encountered by our client while trying to " +
            "communicate with the DynamoDB, " +
        "like being unable to access the network.");
    System.out.println("The Error Message is: " + ac.getMessage());
                                }
```

In the above code, we are using the AWS for java so as to delete an item within the "*try*" block and then a "*catch*" block has been used for us to respond to the error. In our case, the user will be presented with a message that the request has failed. The class "*AmazonServiceException*" has been used for us to retrieve any errors associated with our operation. The class "*AmazonClientException*" has also been used in the example, since the request might fail due to other types of reasons.

Error Retries and Exponential Backoff

For most components which are used on the network such as DNS servers, load-balancers, switches, and others, errors will always be generated whenever operations are being processed. In a networked environment, error responses can easily be handled by implementation of retries on the client side of applications. With this technique, the reliability of the application will be increased, and the operational costs will be highly reduced.

Consider the example given below, which shows how the retry logic can be implemented in an application:

```
cRetry = 0
DO
    retry set to false
    DynamoDB request executed
    IF Exception.errorCode = ProvisionedThroughputExceededException
        retry set to true
    ELSE IF Exception.httpStatusCode = 500
        retry set to true
    ELSE IF Exception.httpStatusCode = 400
        retry set to false
        fix client error (4xx)
    IF retry = true
        wait for (2^cRetry * 50) milliseconds
        cRetry = cRetry + 1
WHILE (retry = true AND cRetry < MaxNumberOfRetries)  // limiting the retries
```

With the above code, we have begun by determining whether the error is a server error, that is, 5xx. If the error is found to be a server, a retry of the request will then be made. For AWS SDK users, you can use *"ClientConfiguration"* class so as to configure or change the settings on how the retry is made. For those who do not use the AWS SDK, once you get the error code 5xx for your request, just retry the original request. If you need to improve the efficiency of your flow control, then you should try to implement an efficient exponential backoff algorithm. What happens with this concept is that there will be longer waits in the consecutive retries for error codes.

Chapter 6- DynamoDB Operations

In dynamoDB, there are numerous operations which are supported. These will be discussed in this chapter.

BatchGetItem

When this operation has been used, the attributes of one or more items are returned from a single or more tables. The primary key attribute is used for identification of the items which have been requested.

With a single operation, up to 16MB of data can be retrieved, and this can have up to 100 items. When the BatchGetItem operation is used, and the response size limit has been exceeded, then the operation will return a partial result. If the provisioned throughput of the table is exceeded or an internal failure occurs during this operation, then the same effect will be experienced as a partial result will be returned to the user. Once this has happened, then a value for *"UnprocessedKeys"* will be returned, and this means that this can be used for performing a retry of the operation. This helps in making the work of the users much easier. The default setting for this method is for it to perform consistent reads of the tables which are contained in the request. Consider the example code given below:

```
{
    "RequestItems":
    {
        "string" :
        {
            "AttributesToObtain": [
                "string"
            ],
            "ConsistentRead": boolean,
            "AttributeNamesofExpression":
            {
                "string" :
                "string"
            },
            "Keys": [
                {
                    "string" :
                    {
                        "B": blob_data,
                        "BOOL": Boolean_data,
                        "BS": [
                            blob
                        ],
                        "L": [
                            ValueofAttribute
                        ],
                        "M":
                        {
                            "string" :
                            ValueofAttribute
                        },
                        "N": "string",
```

```
                    "NS": [
                    "string"
                      ],
                "NULL": boolean,
                 "S": "string",
                    "SS": [
                    "string"
                      ]
                       }
                       }
                      ],
        "ProjectionExpression": "string"
                       }
                      },
          "CapacityConsumed": "string"
                       }
```

The above code just shows the syntax taken by the request. Note that the data which has been specified for the request is in JSON format.

The parameter *"RequestItems"* describes a map of table name(s) and a map describing the item which is to be retrieved from each table is available for each table. A single table name can be used once per each *"BatchGetItem"* request.

Each element which is contained in the map of elements to be retrieved consists of the following:

- ConsistentRead- if this is set to *true,* then a strong consistent read will be done. If set to *false,* then an eventual consistent read will be done. The default setting for this is *false.*

- ExpressionAttributeNames- this is a substitution token(s) for the name attribute and in the parameter *"ProjectionExpression."*

The following is the syntax of the response:

```
{
    "ConsumedCapacity": [
        {
            "CapacityUnits": number_data,
            "GlobalSecondaryIndexes":
            {
                "string" :
                {
                    "CapacityUnits": number_data
                }
            },
            "LocalSecondaryIndexes":
            {
                "string" :
                {
                    "CapacityUnits": number_data
                }
            },
            "Table": {
                "CapacityUnits": number_data
```

```
        },
        "TableName": "string"
    }
],
"Responses":
    {
        "string" :
        [
            {
                "string" :
                {
                    "B": blob_data,
                    "BOOL": Boolean_type,
                    "BS": [
                        blob
                    ],
                    "L": [
                        ValueofAttribute
                    ],
                    "M":
                    {
                        "string" :
                        ValueofAttribute
                    },
                    "N": "string",
                    "NS": [
                        "string"
                    ],
                    "NULL": boolean,
                    "S": "string",
                    "SS": [
                        "string"
```

```
                    ]
                }
            }
        ]
    },
"UnprocessedKeys":
    {
        "string" :
        {
"AttributesToGet": [
            "string"
            ],
"ConsistentRead": boolean,
"ExpressionAttributeNames":
            {
            "string" :
            "string"
            },
        "Keys": [
            {
            "string" :
                {
            "B": blob_data,
            "BOOL": boolean,
                "BS": [
                blob
                ],
                "L": [
        ValueofAttribute
                ],
                "M":
                {
```

```
                    "string" :
                  ValueofAttribute
                        },
                  "N": "string",
                    "NS": [
                    "string"
                        ],
              "NULL": boolean,
                  "S": "string",
                    "SS": [
                    "string"
                        ]
                        }
                        }
                        ],
          "ProjectionExpression": "string"
                        }
                        }
                        }
```

BatchWriteItem

With this operation, multiple elements are put or deleted from a particular table. When this operation is called once, up to 16MB of data can be written or deleted, and this can be made of up to 25 requests. Each item which is to be written or deleted can be of up to 400KB. Note that this operation cannot be used for updating an item. If you need to do this, then use the API *"UpdateItem."* The syntax for the request in this operation is as follows:

```
{
"RequestItems":
{
"string" :
[
{
"DeleteRequest": {
"Key":
{
"string" :
{
"B": blob_data,
"BOOL": boolean,
"BS": [
blob
],
"L": [
ValueofAttribute
],
"M":
```

```
                  {
              "string" :
          ValueofAttribute
                  },
           "N": "string",
            "NS": [
             "string"
                ],
        "NULL": boolean,
          "S": "string",
            "SS": [
             "string"
                ]
                }
                }
                },
        "PutRequest": {
             "Item":
                {
              "string" :
                {
          "B": blob_data,
         "BOOL": boolean,
             "BS": [
               blob
                ],
             "L": [
          ValueofAttribute
                ],
              "M":
                {
             "string" :
```

```
        ValueofAttribute
             },
        "N": "string",
        "NS": [
        "string"
             ],
    "NULL": boolean,
      "S": "string",
        "SS": [
        "string"
             ]
             }
             }
             }
             }
             ]
             },
"ReturnConsumedCapacity": "string",
"ReturnItemCollectionMetrics": "string"
             }
```

Create Table

With this operation, a new table will be added to your account. For those who are using an AWS account, then note that the table name for each region must be unique. This means that one can create tables with the same name in different regions of the account.

The operation *"Create Table"* is an asynchronous operation. Once the DynamoDB receives the request for *"CreateTable,"* it immediately returns a response specifying the *"TableStatus"* of the *"Creating."* Once the creation of the table has been completed, its status will be changed to *"ACTIVE"* by DynamoDB. For you to perform either a read or a write operation on the table, then its status must be set to *"ACTIVE."*

Secondary indexes for the table can be specified in the operation for *"Create Table,"* although this is optional. For the purpose of creating multiple tables which have multiple indexes on them, then the process has to be done sequentially. Secondary indexes are optional, but one can create them if they need to do so. For tables with secondary indexes, only one of them can be in a *"CREATING"* state.

The request syntax is as shown below:

```
{
    "AttributeDefinitions": [
        {
            "NameofAttribute": "string",
            "AttributeType": "string"
        }
    ],
```

```
"GlobalSecondaryIndexes": [
    {
        "IndexName": "string",
        "KeySchema": [
            {
                "NameofAttribute": "string",
                "KeyType": "string"
            }
        ],
        "Projection": {
            "NonKeyAttributes": [
                "string"
            ],
            "ProjectionType": "string"
        },
        "ProvisionedThroughput": {
            "ReadCapacityUnits": number,
            "WriteCapacityUnits": number
        }
    }
],
"KeySchema": [
    {
        "NameofAttribute": "string",
        "KeyType": "string"
    }
],
"LocalSecondaryIndexes": [
    {
        "IndexName": "string",
        "KeySchema": [
            {
```

```
            "NameofAttribute": "string",
            "KeyType": "string"
                }
            ],
        "Projection": {
        "NonKeyAttributes": [
            "string"
            ],
        "ProjectionType": "string"
                }
            }
        ],
    "ProvisionedThroughput": {
    "ReadCapacityUnits": number,
    "WriteCapacityUnits": number
            },
    "StreamSpecification": {
    "StreamEnabled": boolean,
    "StreamViewType": "string"
            },
    "NameofTable": "string"
        }
```

The *"AttributeDefinitions"* is just an array of attributes which make up the primary key for a table or a particular index. The *"keySchema"* is used for specification of the attributes which make up the primary key of the table or an index. The attributes which are contained in this must be specified within the *"AttributeDefinitions"* array. The response syntax should be as shown below:

```json
{
    "TableDescription": {
        "AttributeDefinitions": [
            {
                " NameofAttribute ": "string",
                "AttributeType": "string"
            }
        ],
        "CreationDateTime": number,
        "GlobalSecondaryIndexes": [
            {
                "IndexStatus": "string",
                "Backfilling": boolean,
                "IndexName": "string",
                "ItemCount": number,
                "IndexSizeBytes": number,
                "KeySchema": [
                    {
                        " NameofAttribute ": "string",
                        "KeyType": "string"
                    }
                ],
                "Projection": {
                    "NonKeyAttributes": [
                        "string"
                    ],
                    "ProjectionType": "string"
                },
                "ProvisionedThroughput": {
                    "WriteCapacityUnits": number
                    "LastIncreaseDateTime": number,
                    "NumberOfDecreasesToday": number,
```

```
            "LastDecreaseDateTime": number,
            "ReadCapacityUnits": number,
        }
    }
],
"ItemCount": number,
"KeySchema": [
    {
        "NameofAttribute": "string",
        "KeyType": "string"
    }
],
"LatestStreamLabel": "string",
"LatestStreamArn": "string",
"LocalSecondaryIndexes": [
    {
        "ItemCount": number,
        "IndexArn": "string",
        "IndexSizeBytes": number,
        "IndexName": "string",
        "KeySchema": [
            {
                "AttributeName": "string",
                "KeyType": "string"
            }
        ],
        "Projection": {
            "NonKeyAttributes": [
                "string"
            ],
            "ProjectionType": "string"
        }
```

```
                    }
                    ],
         "ProvisionedThroughput": {
         "ReadCapacityUnits": number,
       "LastDecreaseDateTime": number,
   "NumberOfDecreasesToday": number,
       "LastIncreaseDateTime": number,
        "WriteCapacityUnits": number
                    },
          "StreamSpecification": {
            "StreamEnabled": boolean,
          "StreamViewType": "string"
                    },
         "TableSizeBytes": number,
            "TableArn": "string",
          "TableStatus": "string"
          "TableName": "string",
                    }
                    }
```

DeleteItem

This is used for deleting a single item from the table by use of a primary key. A conditional delete can be performed in which an item which exists will be deleted or the one which has an expected attribute value. Other than performing the delete operation, the attributes of the item can be returned, and this can be done in the same operation. In this case, we use the *"ReturnValues"* attribute. It takes the following request syntax:

```
{
"ConditionExpression": "string",
"ConditionalOperator": "string",
"Expected":
{
"string" :
{
"AttributeValueList": [
{
"B": blob-data,
"BOOL": boolean,
"BS": [
blob
],
"L": [
ValueofAttribute
],
"M":
{
"string" :
ValueofAttribute
```

},
"N": "string",
"NS": [
"string"
],
"NULL": boolean,
"S": "string",
"SS": [
"string"
]
}
],
"ComparisonOperator": "string",
"Exists": boolean,
"Value": {
"B": blob-data,
"BOOL": boolean,
"BS": [
blob
],
"L": [
ValueofAttribute
],
"M":
{
"string" :
ValueofAttribute
},
"N": "string",
"NS": [
"string"
],

```
                    "NULL": boolean,
                      "S": "string",
                       "SS": [
                       "string"
                          ]
                          }
                          }
                         },
         "ExpressionAttributeNames":
                          {
                     "string" :
                     "string"
                         },
        "ExpressionAttributeValues":
                          {
                     "string" :
                          {
                   "B": blob-data,
                  "BOOL": boolean,
                      "BS": [
                       blob
                         ],
                       "L": [
                  ValueofAttribute
                         ],
                       "M":
                          {
                     "string" :
                  ValueofAttribute
                         },
                   "N": "string",
                      "NS": [
```

```
                "string"
              ],
              "NULL": boolean,
              "S": "string",
              "SS": [
                "string"
              ]
            }
          },
          "Key":
          {
            "string" :
            {
              "B": blob-data,
              "BOOL": boolean,
              "BS": [
                blob
              ],
              "L": [
                ValueofAttribute
              ],
              "M":
              {
                "string" :
                ValueofAttribute
              },
              "N": "string",
              "NS": [
                "string"
              ],
              "NULL": boolean,
              "S": "string",
```

"SS": [

"string"

]

}

},

"ReturnItemCollectionMetrics": "string",

"ReturnConsumedCapacity": "string",

"ReturnValues": "string",

"TableName": "string"

}

The parameter *"TableName"* is the name of the table from which we want to delete an item. The *"ConditionExpression"* specifies the condition which has to be satisfied so that the *"DeleteItem"* operation qualifies to be executed.

The response syntax of the method is as follows:

{

"Attributes":

{

"string" :

{

"B": blob-data,

"BOOL": boolean,

"BS": [

blob

],

"L": [

ValueofAttribute

```
                ],
               "M":
                {
              "string" :
          ValueofAttribute
                },
          "N": "string",
            "NS": [
            "string"
                ],
          "NULL": boolean,
           "S": "string",
            "SS": [
            "string"
                ]
                }
                },
      "ConsumedCapacity": {
      "CapacityUnits": number,
   "GlobalSecondaryIndexes":
                {
            "string" :
                {
       "CapacityUnits": number
                }
                },
    "LocalSecondaryIndexes":
                {
            "string" :
                {
       "CapacityUnits": number
                }
```

```
        },
        "Table": {
            "CapacityUnits": number
        },
        "TableName": "string"
    },
    "ItemCollectionMetrics": {
        "ItemCollectionKey":
        {
            "string" :
            {
                "B": blob-data,
                "BOOL": boolean,
                "BS": [
                    blob
                ],
                "L": [
                    ValueofAttribute
                ],
                "M":
                {
                    "string" :
                    ValueofAttribute
                },
                "N": "string",
                "NS": [
                    "string"
                ],
                "NULL": boolean,
                "S": "string",
                "SS": [
                    "string"
```

```
              ]
            }
          },
"SizeEstimateRangeGB": [
          number
              ]
            }
          }
```

Delete Table

With this operation, the table together with its items is deleted. Once the *"DeleteTable"* request has been issued, the status of the table will be changed to *"DELETING"* until the DynamoDB completes the operation. The deletion can also be done even when the table is in the *"ACTIVE"* state. However, if you issue the *"DeleteTable"* request and then the table is found to be in a *"CREATING"* or *"UPDATING"* status, the request will return an exception, meaning that your request cannot be serviced. An exception will also be returned if the table is not found. If the table is found to be in the *"DELETING"* state, no error will be returned.

The operation takes the following request syntax:

```
{
"TableName": "string"
}
```

The *"TableName"* parameter is the name of the table which is to be deleted.

Describe Table

When this operation is used, the information about the table is returned. The information is this case is all about the status that the table is currently at, the primary key schema for the table, and indexes if present on the table. However, it is not recommended that you issue this operation immediately after issuing the *"CreateTable"* request. If you do this, you might get an exception as the return. The reason for this is because the metadata for the table might not be created and hence not available. You should wait for some seconds before running this operation.

The Request syntax for this operation is as follows:

```
{
"TableName": "string"
}
```

The parameter *"TableName"* is the name of the table which we need to describe. It should have a minimum of 3 characters and a maximum of 255 characters, and if you violate this requirement, then you will get an error as the result. The response syntax for this operation is as follows:

```
{
"Table": {
"AttributeDefinitions": [
{
"NameofAttribute": "string",
"AttributeType": "string"
}
```

```json
        ],
    "CreationDateTime": number,
    "GlobalSecondaryIndexes": [
        {
            "ItemCount": number,
            "Backfilling": boolean,
            "IndexName": "string",
            "IndexArn": "string",
            "IndexSizeBytes": number,
            "IndexStatus": "string",
            "KeySchema": [
                {
                    " NameofAttribute ": "string",
                    "KeyType": "string"
                }
            ],
            "Projection": {
                "NonKeyAttributes": [
                    "string"
                ],
                "ProjectionType": "string"
            },
            "ProvisionedThroughput": {
                "ReadCapacityUnits": number,
                "NumberOfDecreasesToday": number,
                "LastDecreaseDateTime": number,
                "LastIncreaseDateTime": number,
                "WriteCapacityUnits": number
            }
        }
    ],
    "ItemCount": number,
```

```
        "KeySchema": [
             {
    " NameofAttribute ": "string",
        "KeyType": "string"
             }
        ],
    "LatestStreamLabel": "string",
    "LatestStreamArn": "string",
    "LocalSecondaryIndexes": [
             {
    "IndexSizeBytes": number,
        "IndexArn": "string",
        "IndexName": "string",
        "ItemCount": number,
        "KeySchema": [
             {
    " NameofAttribute ": "string",
        "KeyType": "string"
             }
        ],
        "Projection": {
        "NonKeyAttributes": [
             "string"
        ],
        "ProjectionType": "string"
             }
             }
        ],
    "ProvisionedThroughput": {
    "ReadCapacityUnits": number,
    "LastDecreaseDateTime": number,
    "NumberOfDecreasesToday": number,
```

```
        "LastIncreaseDateTime": number,
        "WriteCapacityUnits": number
      },
      "StreamSpecification": {
        "StreamEnabled": boolean,
        "StreamViewType": "string"
      },
      "TableSizeBytes": number,
      "TableArn": "string",
      "TableName": "string",
      "TableStatus": "string"
    }
  }
```

Consider the sample request which is given below:

```
POST / HTTP/1.1
Host: dynamodb.<region>.<domain>;
X-Amz-Date: <Date>
Authorization: ADS4-HNBC-SHA256 Credential=<Credential>,
SignedHeaders=<Headers>, Signature=<Signature>
User-Agent: <UserAgentString>
x-amz-content-sha256: <PayloadHash>
Content-Type: application/x-amz-json-1.0
Content-Length: <PayloadSizeBytes>
Connection: Keep-Alive X-Amz-Target:
DynamoDB_20120810.DescribeTable
{
```

```
"TableName":"myTable"
}
```

In the above case, we just need to describe a table named *"myTable,"* and all of its attributes will be presented to us.

Chapter 7 - Getting Data from DynamoDB

Once you have saved your data into the DynamoDB database, you might need to access the data for using it. This can easily be done by use of its key. Consider the example given below:

```
from skill.dynamodb2.table import Table
students= Table('students')
joeljohn = students.get_item(username='joeljohn, last_name='john')
```

In the above case, we want to access the data for a student whose username is *"joeljohn,"* and whose last name is *"john."*

Once you have an instance of the item, a dictionary-like interface to the data will be presented. This is shown below:

```
# Reading a field out.
>>>joeljohn ['first_name']
'Joel'
```

```
# Changing a field (DOESN'T SAVE YET!).
>>> joeljohn['first_name'] = 'Mercy'
# Deleting the data from it (DOESN'T SAVE YET!).
>>> del joeljohn ['account_type']
```

That is how it can be done.

How to update an Item

Once you have created your items in DynamoDB, you might need to change or update them. Consider the example which is given below:

```
>>> from skill.dynamodb2.table import Table
>>> myTable = Table('myTable')
>>> joeljohn = myTable.get_item(username='joeljohn', last_name='Doe')
>>> joeljohn['first_name'] = 'Johann'
>>> joeljohn['whatever'] = "Hey, I think it is your own wish"
>>> del joeljohn['account_type']
# this will affect all of the fields, including the ones which have not been
locally chaned.
>>> joeljohn.save()
True
```

In the above case, we have just send the data to the DynamoDB, and we have assumed that nothing about the data has been changed since reading it.

It is possible for someone to overwrite the data. This should only happen if you are very sure that the new version of the data that you currently have is the correct one. This is known as a full overwrite, and it can be done as follows:

```
joeljohn = myTable.get_item(username='joeljohn', last_name='john')
joeljohn['first_name'] = 'Mercy'
```

```
joeljohn['whatever'] = " Hey, I think it is your own wish "
```
Specify ``overwrite=True`` for a full replacement of the data.
```
joeljohn.save(overwrite=True)
True
```

That is how simply it can be done. Note that in the above case, we have force overwritten the data. A partial update of data items is also supported in DynamoDB. This happens when the changes have been done only to certain fields and not all of the fields. In this case, you just have to send the data to the changed fields so as to update their values. The rest of the fields will remain untouched. Consider the example given below which shows how this can be done:

```
joeljohn = users.get_item(username='joeljohn', last_name='john')
joeljohn['first_name'] = 'Mercy'
joeljohn['whatever'] = " Hey, I think it is your own wish "
del joeljohn['account_type']
```
This is a partial update, affecting only the
``first_name/whatever/account_type`` fields.
```
joeljohn.partial_save()
True
```

With the above, you will have performed a partial update of the data item.

Deletion of an Item

Items which have been added into the table can be deleted. There are two ways how this can be done.

In the first case, if you have an instance of the item which is already running, you can just call the method *"Item.delete."* This is shown below:

>>> joeljohn.delete()
True

It might be possible that you have the instance of the item running, but you might not want to incur the above call. In this case, you can do it as shown below:

from skill.dynamodb2.table import Table
myTable = Table('myTable')
myTable.delete_item(username='joeljohn', last_name='john')
True

Batch Writing

With this process, the process of writing is sped up, and the number of written requests that are sent to the DynamoDB are highly reduced. It should be used in situations whereby there is a large amount of data which is to be written to the database. In this case, the calls that you need to make are wrapped into the call manager. The following example illustrates how the call manager can be used:

```
import time
from skill.dynamodb2.table import Table
myTable = Table('myTable')
with myTable.batch_write() as batch:
    batch.put_item(data={
        'username': 'markjoel',
        'first_name': 'Mark',
        'last_name': 'Joel',
        'date_joined': int(time.time()),
    })
    batch.put_item(data={
        'username': 'titusfrancis',
        'first_name': 'Titus',
        'last_name': 'Francis',
        'date_joined': int(time.time()),
    })
    batch.delete_item(username='mercyjohn', last_name='john')
```

That is how batch writing can be done in DynamoDB.

Querying

In the case of databases having large data sets, fetching a single item at a time can be tedious. If you are in need of fetching multiple records, then a standard query can be used or query via a local secondary index or even perform a scan of the entire table. Consider the example given below:

```python
from skill.dynamodb2.fields import HashKey, RangeKey, GlobalAllIndex
from skill.dynamodb2.table import Table
from skill.dynamodb2.types import NUMBER
import time
myTable = Table.create('myTable2', schema=[
    HashKey('account_type'),
    RangeKey('last_name'),
], throughput={
    'read': 5,
    'write': 15,
}, global_indexes=[
    GlobalAllIndex('DateJoinedIndex', parts=[
        HashKey('account_type'),
        RangeKey('date_joined', data_type=NUMBER),
    ],
    throughput={
        'read': 1,
        'write': 1,
    }),
])
```

Below is the data:

```python
with myTable.batch_write() as batch:
    batch.put_item(data={
        'account_type': 'standard_user',
        'first_name': 'Joel',
        'last_name': 'John',
        'is_owner': True,
        'email': True,
        'date_joined': int(time.time()) - (60*60*1),
    })
    batch.put_item(data={
        'account_type': 'standard_user',
        'first_name': 'Mercy',
        'last_name': 'John',
        'date_joined': int(time.time()) - 2,
    })
    batch.put_item(data={
        'account_type': 'standard_user',
        'first_name': 'Mark',
        'last_name': 'Joel',
        'date_joined': int(time.time()) - (60*60*2),
    })
    batch.put_item(data={
        'account_type': 'super_user',
        'first_name': 'Daniel',
        'last_name': 'Geoffrey',
        'is_owner': True,
        'email': True,
```

```
            'date_joined': int(time.time()) - 1,
        })
```

Once you execute the above, you will have back your results. They can then be used for multiple requests sent to DynamoDB, since they will be presented in pages.

Suppose you want to execute a query for all of the *"first_names"* which begin with the letter *"J."* This can be done as follows:

```
names_with_j = myTable.query_2(
account_type__eq='standard_user',
last_name__beginswith='J'
)
for myTable in names_with_j:
    print myTable['first_name']
'John'
'Joel'
'Mercy'
```

The results can also be reversed or limited as shown below:

```
rev_with_j = myTable.query_2(
account_type__eq='standard_user',
first_name__beginswith='J',
reverse=True,
limit=2
```

```
)
for myTable in rev_with_j:
print myTable['first_name']
'Mercy'
'Joel'
```

Conclusion

It can be concluded that DynamoDB is a NoSQL database which is proprietarily provided by Amazon. When compared to other NoSQL databases, the implementation of DynamoDB is very different, but its underlying data model is very similar to the others. The multi-master design of the database makes it easy for database clients to resolve conflicts which may arise. The database uses synchronous replication if multiple and different datacenters are to be used. With DynamoDB, unlike in other types of Amazon products, the purchase of its services is based on the throughput as opposed to using storage. Note that for the database to be scaled, the process has to be done manually. Whenever the client machines request for much or large throughput from the DynamoDB, it handles this by using solid-state drives in which the data and the traffic are spread out into different servers.

This is why the performance of DynamoDB is very predictable. The database can be integrated with other software such as the Hadoop. With DynamoDB, one can choose to set up the DynamoDB local, in which case they will have to install it into their local systems. They can also choose to use the DynamoDB which is provided by Amazon, and the experience will be similar. For you to write data, you can do it item by item or do it in multiple records. In the latter case, the process is known as batch writing, and it saves time and makes the overall work a bit easier. The same case applies to querying the database, in which one can query for a single record or for multiple records. Note that the primary key is the one used for searching for individual items which have been inserted into the database.

This is because it uniquely identifies a particular record. You need to carry out these operations. Whenever requests fail in DynamoDB, one is encouraged to retry until they succeed.

Made in the USA
Coppell, TX
21 December 2019